Dog Tricks

Best smart dog tricks to teach your dog in record time

ANTHONY PORTOKALOGLOU

Copyright © 2017 by Anthony Portokaloglou
All rights reserved. No part of this publication may be reproduced, distributed or transmitted in any form or by any means, without prior written permission from the author.

Disclaimer Notice

The techniques described in this book are for informational purposes only. All attempts have been made by the author to provide real and accurate content. No responsibility will be taken by the author for any damages cost by misuse of the content described in this book. Please consult a licensed professional before utilizing the information of this book.

I hope you will enjoy my book. I would be very grateful if you would consider leaving a review on Amazon. Thank you!

Introduction: 5

Chapter One – General Training Tips 6

Chapter Two – Training with a clicker 10

Chapter Three – Teaching Kisses........................... 13

Chapter Four – Bark on Command..........................16

Chapter Five – Shake Hands 19

Chapter Six – Fetch 22

Chapter Seven – Roll Over 25

Chapter Eight - Play Dead / or Shoot the Dog 29

Chapter Nine – Spin 32

Chapter Ten – Stand on Hind Legs 35

Chapter Eleven – Sit Pretty 40

Chapter Twelve – Hug 43

Chapter Thirteen – High Five 48

Chapter Fourteen- Army Crawl 51

Chapter Fifteen - Collect garbage ....……54

Chapter Sixteen – Skateboard 57

Chapter Seventeen – Handstand 60

Chapter Eighteen - Back Up 63

Chapter Nineteen - Open and close doors 66

Chapter Twenty - Fetch a drink from the Fridge.......... 69

Chapter Twenty-One – Beg 73

Chapter Twenty-two – Teaching Your Dog to Find It…...76

Chapter Twenty-three – Dance 79

Introduction:

People are amazed when house-pets can do specialty tricks, are obedient, and a pleasure to be around. Any pet can be taught how to do several tricks, it simply takes patience, consistency and lots of love and affection for your pet. If you desire to have a pet that is enjoyable to be around, obeys, and is fun to show off to your friends; then read on! Dog Tricks: Best smart dog tricks to teach your dog in record time is exactly what you have been looking for!

Chapter One – General Training Tips

- Be liberal with your attention and affection.

Everyone, including pets, love attention and affection. Too many pet owners are liberal with their displeasure or correction and stingy with their praise. It should be the opposite. When your dog is behaving well make sure you give your pet lots of praise and affirmation of that good behavior. Tell him he's a good dog and you can even go over the top with praise when your dog has pleased you, and it's a good thing! You can never give your pet too much praise or too much love.

- Listen to your pet.

You pet may not be social with other dogs, or may be social with dogs but apprehensive around people. Pay attention to your pet's idiosyncrasies, don't insist your pet interact when they are obviously not comfortable; it could cause an unwanted situation or possibly pet problems down the road. Just like people have personalities and characteristics – pets do as well. It is not that they cannot be modified, but be aware of what they are in the training process for a happier training experience for both you and your pet.

- Be clear in your commands.

It is oftentimes not enough just to say "no" to your pet. Let's say he is jumping on something or someone, don't just say "no"; but you may want to say "no" and then command that he "sit". Make sure your pet understands what you are expecting him to do or not do. Remember although animals can learn hundreds of human words and phrases, they do not understand as a human does. They are easily confused. That is why you must be clear and concise. In order to get the same behavior, you must do the same command or signal.

- You MUST be consistent.

Commands need to be uniform. If more than one person is dealing with the pet, then everyone needs to use the same commands. If your pet is jumping on furniture and you are using the "down" command and someone else is saying "get off" your pet will have difficulty learning what is expected. If you correct a dog for a behavior one time and then let him get by with it another time it is unkind and unfair; and inconsistent behavior will extend the training time. The golden rule of pet training is that you MUST be consistent!

- Be realistic in your expectations.

To change behavior, you must understand that you will invest time. You will repeat commands over and over. You will need patience. Often normal dog behavior such as digging, jumping, barking will take the most time to change. The longer a dog is allowed bad behavior the longer it will take to correct it, that is why training as a puppy is so much easier than an older canine. It is never too late to change the behavior some will just take longer than others, so be realistic.

- Nutrition is very important.

Insure your dog has a high-quality diet with the right amounts of protein. If you have a sedentary dog that is confined to smaller living quarters you would not give him the same amount as a dog that is working with cattle all day. Cheating on a quality diet for your dog will just insure that you have vet bills in the future and a shorter life span for your friend. A veterinarian is a good resource to help you develop the right diet for your pet.

- Your dog will behave in what is reinforced, not necessarily what you want.

If you dog is doing something you really don't care for, then it is more likely that it is a behavior that has been reinforced in the past. Let's say a dog gets a toy and barks so that you throw it. If you throw the toy, he understands that barking will get you to play. If you say "no" and he consistently barks and then you throw the toy, you have reinforced that excessive barking and persistence will get him his way. Before long, your dog will be barking to get his way. So, what do you do? Ignore his barking and do not throw the toy until he has stopped. Or give him an alternate command such as "sit" or "down" before throwing his toy.

- Treats and Rewards

Using treats is a proven effective way to encourage good behavior in dogs. But, you are not limited to treats. Use the surroundings around you and each interaction with your pet is a learning and teaching opportunity. Use praise, touch, loving inflection in your voice, games, walks, and play time. Remember the behavior should produce the treat, the treat should not produce the behavior!

- Earning Freedom.

It is wise to confine your dog to a crate, a room, or an area and let them earn freedom as they mature and show they can be responsible enough not to destroy things. Some common mistakes pet owners make is giving too much freedom too quickly. Too much freedoms leads to things getting torn up, accidents, and bad behavior. A crate is a great way to give your pet a safe space and to restrict your pet. If a crate isn't possible a child gate or dog proof room can be helpful.

Chapter Two – Training with a clicker

Clicker training is an awesome, science-based technique to commune with your dog. Some feel that it is easier than standard command-based training techniques.

Tips and Ideas

- The clicker has a two-toned sound. Push and release the clicker and then treat with a delicious treat that your pet loves!
- When you pet is doing a desired behavior, click then. Timing is important. If you pet stops the behavior at the sound of the click, that is fine. Give the treat after and that is fine.
- When your dog does something you like, you can click. Ideas would be coming towards you, following an object, etc.
- It is important to only click once. I f you desire to show enthusiasm increase praise or number of treats – not the number of clicks.
- Work in short increments. Do not do long training sessions.
- Click for good behavior. If your puppy relieves himself in the proper spot then click the good behavior. Click for silence instead of scolding for making noises. When the leash is slack then click and treat, not when the dog is pulling.

- If your pet is heading in the right direction of behavior, but hasn't got it completely down; click for the movement in the right direction.
- Keep raising expectations. When you have a good response in one area then continue to ask for more. This technique is called "shaping" a behavior.
- When your pet has learned to do something for clicks, he will begin demonstrating that behavior spontaneously trying to get you to click – now is the time to add cues such as a word or hand signal. Begin to click for behavior if it happens during or after the cue. Ignore the behavior if the cue is not given.
- You don't order your pet around; clicker training is not command-based. When your pet is not responding it is not disobeying it just needs to fully learn the cue. Find additional ways to cue and then click for the desired behavior. Work in a quiet place with as few distractions as possible.
- If you find yourself frustrated put the clicker away. You cannot combine scolding, leash jerking in tandem with clicker training. You will lose your pet's confidence in the clicker and maybe even in you.
- Clicker training is oftentimes done with pets that are going to learn complex tricks. It is a wonderful way to enrich your relationship with any pet, but definitely not the only way

to train. There are many ways to effectively train your pet!

Chapter Three – Teaching Kisses

Items that will come in handy for teaching your dog to kiss is peanut butter or coconut oil, both are healthy for your dog. A towel would also be a helpful item if your dog is known for drooling.

Training Tips:

- Place a small dab of the peanut butter or coconut oil on your cheek (or the location you prefer kisses).
- Give a cue phrase such as: Give Me a Kiss, Give Kisses, Give Me Sugar, etc.
- Lean towards your puppy. He will be happy to lick the yummy treat from your cheek or the location you have selected.
- Do this training procedure several times a day and before you know it you will be getting kisses each and every time you say the command!

Alternate Training Tip:

- Each time your dog licks you, give the command "give kisses".
- You can also use a clicker to mark the action, just click the clicker each time your dog licks you.
- When he kisses you tell him "good job" and reward him with a treat. Before long, your dog will be kissing on command, and all you

had to do was reward him for his natural behavior.

<u>Caution:</u>

Some dogs will be very exuberant, and in teaching them to kiss it may be difficult to get them to stop. It would be wise to give him a stop command such as "enough" or "stop". When your dog is kissing you give him the stop command of your choice. When he stops licking tell him he is a good dog and reward him with a treat. Do this each time you receive kisses and you will be able to control the number of kisses that you receive.

On occasion, a dog will be averse to getting near the face, if that is the case you can teach your dog to kiss the back of your hand instead. Some dogs are intimidated greatly by close proximity to the eyes; and you need to determine if your dog is comfortable or not with face kisses.

<u>Food for thought:</u> Not everyone likes kisses from a dog, and not everyone will appreciate the affection. Get permission before having your dog kiss someone other than yourself!

Chapter Four – Bark on Command

There are basically four steps in teaching your dog to bark on command. It is beneficial to teach your dog to speak on cue as it will be easier to teach your dog to be quiet on cue as well. You also can reward your dog for just one bark instead of barking non-stop for several minutes.

Training Tips:

- First, find something that gets your dog excited enough to bark. This could be a favorite toy or treat. If that doesn't work, perhaps having someone knock on the door or ring a doorbell.
- Wave the object around and get excited giving the verbal command "speak".
- As soon as your pet barks, then mark that behavior immediately by praise and a treat, or giving him the toy. If you are using the clicker method of training, then you can click and treat.
- As your dog starts consistently offering a bark, you can add a hand signal or can continue to use the speak command.

<u>Caution:</u>

Do not reward barking if you have not asked your dog to speak.

Attempt to capture only a single bark. You do not want "speak" to indicate non-stop barking.

Food for Thought:
You can teach "speak" so that your dog can alert you that he needs to go outside. By teaching "speak" and rewarding for the cued behavior, you can also modify that concept and teach your dog to bark softer or to be quiet on command as well.

Chapter Five – Shake Hands

You will need your pet in a sitting position, so a prerequisite for this trick is that you have already taught your dog to sit.

Training Tips:

- Hold a treat in your hand and let him see the treat, then close your fist over the treat.
- Use your finger and lightly tap on the back of your dog's paw, right under this dew claw. When he lifts his foot away, sweep your hand forward and pick up his paw. (If you are doing clicker training you will want to click at this time).
- Give him the treat and praise him.
- Keep doing this until your dog starts to lift his foot as soon as you reach toward it, now you can also add a verbal cue such as the work "shake".
- Dogs are not able to generalize easily, so just because he can shake with one paw, will not automatically make him able to shake with the other paw. If that is your desire, do the same steps, but with a different cue word for his other paw.

Food for Thought:

Practice in short increments of five minutes so that neither one of you get frustrated. Always end a session on a positive note. If your pet isn't getting it, go back to a trick he does know and reward him for that. Make sure your treats can be eaten quickly or time will be wasted watching him chew.

Chapter Six – Fetch

It would seem like teaching a pet how to fetch would be the easiest trick in the world to teach since dogs both love playing and pleasing their owners and fetch involves both of these; but sometimes this trick is the most difficult to master!
There are some dogs that will automatically get the general idea that you wish them to chase and retrieve the object thrown, most don't. They will sit and stare at you wondering why you decided to toss away a perfectly good toy, or they happily chase after it and then engage you in a rousing game of "keep away".
Training Tips:
- Begin with Chasing
- If your pup just sits, then your first objective is to teach him to chase the object. This can be accomplished by offering him treats, affection or play – depending on what motivates your particular dog.
- Regardless of the motivation used, you want to encourage your dog to go after the item you wish for him to fetch. When the dog grabs it, then reward him and take the object away. Repeat several times. Then toss the object a short distance away and reward him immediately when he goes after it. Just repeat until the dog is successfully chasing the item tossed.

- After chasing you want to work on retrieval. You can use two toys to accomplish this. Once he has caught the first toy, offer him the second toy which will get him accustomed to coming back to you. Remember to give the command to "fetch".
- Some dogs just want to play "keep away" and have no interest in "fetching". To help this dog have understanding tie a long rope on his collar. Throw the toy within range of the rope. After the dog has retrieved the toy, pull him gently back to you with the command "fetch".
- When the dog returns whether on his own or by you gently tugging him back, give the command drop it. Drop a treat when you say the command. Generally, a dog will let go of the toy to grab the treat.
- Play this several times so that your dog begins to understand that you will throw the toy again. As he notices a pattern, this game will probably end up being one of his and your favorites!

<u>Food for Thought:</u>
Your dog will not chase after something unless it is actually wanted. Find the toy that motivates your particular dog to fetch whether it be balls, frisbee, sticks, stuffed toys, or bones.

Chapter Seven – Roll Over

To teach a dog to roll over they must first know how to lie down. If you have not yet trained your dog to lie down here are some tips:

Training Tips:

- In a quiet place without distractions have your dog to sit.
- Holding a treat near your dog's nose say "down" and bring your hand slowly straight down to the ground between his paws.
- If he sinks down immediately praise and reward him with the treat. If he doesn't sink down keep the treat in your hand and give him time. You can gently use the other hand to push him into the down position.
- Repeat several times.
- Gradually make it more challenging by adding duration (time spent down) distance (you are moving away) and distractions (toys or conversation with others).

Rolling Over:

- Have his favorite treats on hand already broken into small bits (you don't want him filling up before the training session is over as you want him motivated).
- This is a good trick to use the clicker on.

- Do not reprimand or punish your dog when training him to do tricks. Only use positive reinforcement.
- Train in a quiet, distraction free area. Allow for plenty of floor space.
- Command your dog to lie down. He should be on his stomach with his paws in front of him.
- Hold a treat next to your dog's face in proximity where he can both see and smell it. Make sure your fingers are closed around the treat so that he can't steal it before the trick is completed.
- Move the treat and say, "roll over". Rotate the treat up and around the dog's head to that his nose can follow the treat. Where the nose goes, it stands to reason the head and body usually follow. If you lead your dog's nose along a path that will cause him to roll over as it is followed you will have been successful. Continue to say roll over during this process. If you dog is partially over, you can assist him by pushing his paws the rest of the way over with your free hand.
- The principle is to get your dog to associate the command "roll over" with the physical move of rolling over.
- Keep rewarding throughout the process, if you wait for 100% success your pet may get frustrated. So, give him treats for the small

victories as well. Make sure your voice is friendly and that you are giving a great deal of praise.

- Initially reward your dog every time he successfully rolls over. As time goes on intersperse treats with verbal praise. You don't want him to only do a trick when you have a treat to offer.
- Keep practicing the trick until the dog is able to do the trick without help. You should not have to move the treat, or help him complete the roll with your free hand. (carefully holding the back and front leg and rolling the body without twisting. Grabbing one leg could cause too much pressure on that joint). Helping your dog go over will show him what your goal is.
- Once the trick is mastered then use a less appealing treat, verbal praise, and change things up otherwise your dog will only do tricks when you have a treat in your hand.

Food for Thought:

Frequently people go too fast and try to get the roll over quickly. If you and your pet are struggling, keep trying a series of smaller steps. Some breeds are very suspicious and to expose their underside requires trust. Make sure that you and your pet have a very trusting bond if you find a lot of resistance to this trick. Maybe move on to other tricks and come back to this one as you and your pet grow to trust each other more.

Lay down

Roll Over

Chapter Eight - Play Dead / or Shoot the Dog

Before teaching your pet to do the "shoot the dog dead" trick you your pet will need to have some level of obedience training prior. Your pet will need to obey the down command and it will be helpful if your pet also understands the stay command as well. These two commands will need to be mastered before teaching your pet to play dead.

Training Tips

- Start with the side roll. Have your dog into the down position and have him stay. They gently roll your dog onto a side position and give him the stay command. You may need to hold him down for a little bit just so that he gets the idea of what you are requesting.
- When you release him, give a yummy treat and lots and lots of praise. You will need to practice this initial step in short, two or three minutes sessions a few times a day. Keep it consistent as dogs will train better when training is consistent.
- When your pet is good, then add a verbal cue. Choose which word suits you best for the trick. "Bang, Pow, Boom, or Bang, Your Dead" are all worthy options. Whatever you pick just stay consistent and only use that word.

- Once your pet understands the verbal cue, add a visual cue to the mix. Make a gun with your right index finger and thumb and quickly say your command word.
- This trick generally takes a couple of weeks of consistent practice to master.

<u>Food for Thought:</u>
There are ways to further advance this trick. After you and your pet get the basics of the play dead trick down pat, you can move to make the trick a little more complex to really amaze your friends and family. This could involve something as simple as teaching your dog to play dead from a standing position; a command that may require you to lead him to perform the down command along the way. You could teach your dog to get into the death scene by hamming it up a bit as well. Once your pet has the routine down, you and your pet can have some extra fun!

Chapter Nine – Spin

Spinning is a fun and easy trick to teach your dog. It is important that your pet is paying attention and making eye contact.

Training Tips:

- Get your pets attention, using a treat.
- Then holding the treat in your hand hold it just above his nose and slowly move the treat in a large circle (do this just above his head) in a counter clock wise motion. He should follow your hand.
- Keep moving your hand in a full-circle and if your pet follows your hand to complete the circle, praise him and then give him a treat.
- Keep repeating the above steps getting him familiar with these movements.
- Once your pet is following your hand, then add in the verbal cue "spin around".
- Once your pet has mastered one full spin, then you can add more spins before treating him.
- Once your pet has the idea of this then use the hand motions minus the treat. Ask for two to three spins before giving him a treat.
- Keep these training sessions short and make sure that you end on a good note. You want training time to be a fun time for both you and your pet!

Food for Thought:
Make sure the training area is free from distractions. Other people and pets can hinder the effectiveness of your training time.
Make sure that you have ample room. A dog cannot learn this trick easily in a congested area. Make sure there is ample space for your dog to spin.

Chapter Ten – Stand on Hind Legs

Program One

Before teaching your dog this trick, be aware that standing tall on his hind legs is not natural behavior or a natural position; it may not be comfortable especially for a large breed dog. Smaller dogs generally do better with this trick.

A word of caution: if your dog has any hips issues or a history of hip injury then this would not be a trick to teach your pet. The wellbeing of your pet is certainly more important than any trick. This trick would also be easily done with a clicker.

Be prepared with some great treats, and then your dog will know that great rewards come to those who stand on their hind legs.

Training Tips:
- Start your dog in a sitting position. Then place a treat above your dog's head. After that, move your hand upward and towards your dog's back. The objective is to get your dog's front legs off the ground. As soon as this transpires, then reward your dog

- promptly. Continue to give your dog treats while gradually moving the treat higher up.
- Next and final goal is to get your dog to stand tall on the tips of his toes. Make sure he doesn't put his paws on you for balance, but learns to balance himself.
- Do this routine at least twenty times over the course of several days. Your dog should be comfortable before going to program two.
- Practice this exercise at least twenty times. Your dog should be comfortable in this position before moving on.

Program Two

- Once you can easily persuade your dog into a stand tall position, your next step will be to familiarize him with a hand signal. You do not want him dependent on you having a treat above his head to do his trick.
- The simplest method to do this step is to create a pattern which means three lures followed by one hand signal or voice command. This system is ideal because it automatically sets your dog up for victory. He will anticipate what you want it to do, and he will stand tall

even though you don't have a treat to give him.

- In the beginning, make your hand signals identical to your lure. Basically, this is the same motion as your lure but without any food inside.
- While making sure that your dog is successful and being rewarded for each success, you can begin to slowly make changes to your hand signal. Something like pointing your index finger up.
- Get the hand signal exactly as you would like to have it and work with that particular signal. You can watch yourself in a mirror to see exactly what your pet is seeing, and then make sure you duplicate that motion each and every time you are training.

Program Three

- Once your dog is familiar with the hand signal, then begin conditioning to a verbal command. Saying your verbal command just before you do your hand signal will accomplish this, just make sure you leave a significant pause so that your dog will learn which voice command triggers the hand signal.

- New trainers often make the mistake of saying the command at the same time that they give a hand signal. Give your verbal command such as, "stand", then give the hand signal. Do this at least twenty times. Make sure you significantly pause to avoid confusion in your commands.
- Keep practicing until your pet will stand at either the verbal command or the hand signal. Remember to celebrate each victory with lots of praise, treats, and affirmation!
- Trick training should be a fun time and a time of bonding for both the pet and the owner. If you are getting stressed or frustrated; stop. Do a trick that your pet knows well, give him a treat and call it a day. If you pet is getting bored or anxious; stop. Do a trick your pet knows well, give him a treat and call it a day.

<u>Food for Thought</u>
This is an impressive trick to teach your dog. It is remarkable and your friends and family will be quite impressed. Even though it is a simple trick to teach, your dog will be hailed as a genius!

Chapter Eleven – Sit Pretty

Sitting pretty is cute trick that is just moderate in difficulty to teach. The trick that will need to be mastered before teaching this trick is "sit". So, if your pet can sit, then your pet is ready to "sit pretty". This is a great trick for clicker use. All you will need are some treats and ample space for your dog to move. Most people do not like for a dog to beg for scraps from the table or for treats, but sitting pretty is a cute little trick that looks like they are begging and is both fun and comical to teach. This trick is also a building block for other tricks. You can have your pet act like they are praying, to reach up towards the sky if you make a hand gun gesture, etc. This trick will strengthen their back legs, and makes this good exercise as well as a fun trick.

Training Tips:

- Make sure you start out slowly and build endurance as your dog strengthens. You don't want your pet to end up with sore muscles because you overdid the training.
- You will want to get down to your dog's level while your dog is sitting in front of you.
- Then you will let your pet smell the treat in your hand a lift it above him slowly.
- When the paws lift off of the ground you can click and treat.
- Each time his hindquarters are on the floor and the front paws are up say the command "sit pretty".

- This can be repeated four or five times per training session.

<u>Food for Thought:</u>
Even though this is usually an easy trick to teach not every dog will fall into this category. If you preserve and stay consistent then your dog will soon be sitting pretty. Some dogs may not have the muscle strength to sit pretty. You can help support your dog in the beginning by holding his front paws until he can gain strength. Expect him to hold that position for a few seconds and then give him a hand to rest on. As your pet continues to perform this trick he will gain strength and will be able to do this trick completely on his own. This trick is a great tool for strengthening your pet's hindquarters!

Chapter Twelve – Hug

Section One: Hugging an Object
The hug may just very well be the cutest trick of all time as there is nothing more adorable that a dog that will give you a hug or that can hug his toys! I mean, who doesn't love hugs?
Before teaching your dog to hug, you will need have taught your pet to "sit pretty".
If your dog only knows how to sit in the regular way, then you will end up with a 1-armed hug. If you have trained your dog to "sit pretty" then you should have no difficulty getting both of your pets "arms" around an object or around you!
Training Tips:

- First you will need to get your pet to raise their paw and touch your hand. This can be done in several ways, but shaping or capturing is probably easiest. Just as in humans, most dogs have a dominant paw, and to use your pets dominant paw will make this trick easier to perform. You can give a voice command cue such as "paw" for this step or use the clicker.
- Paw an object – once your pet can paw your hand consistently, you will start introducing and object to his paw. This can be a small toy, paper, or even a small book. This step is to get your pet proficient at pawing a specific

target. Make sure you reward with treats and praise.

- Once your pet is comfortable pawing a variety of objects change up the object using something long and thin such as a dowel rod or broom handle with you holding the top of the item. Make sure that the item is the right size for your dog as they are going to need to balance it and if it is too heavy or big that will not work.
- Wrap the paw – Once your pet has gained comfort in pawing the object then help him by carefully pushing the item towards your dog so he can wrap his paw around it. Make sure you treat and praise as soon as this is successfully accomplished. This step may take some time and patience, so if you find yourself getting aggravated or your pet is getting frustrated, stop. You can resume another time. But, with practice, your pet will eventually hold the item above the ground.
- Strengthening the hold – Now that your dog is comfortable wrapping her paw around the handle you are going to slowly try and pull the object away from him. You are attempting to engage your pet's opposition reflex and have him hand on harder to the object. Start out doing this just briefly and build up the amount of time slowly.

- Removing the rod – Once your pet is adept at holding the object (dowel rod, broom handle, etc.) that is touching the floor, you want to switch out to a light object that your pet can hold the weight of the item. It will take time and some muscle so work in brief increments of time to build up strength. During this part of the process you will want to add the word "hug" into the mix.
- It is even more fun to have your dog catch and then hug a light weight toy.

Food for Thought:
This trick requires your pet to have good balance and strong muscles, so ask your vet if you are unsure whether your dog is physically able to perform this trick. Never force your dog into position or make them hold it for longer than they can do on their own. If your goal is to get a two-handed hug, then you may need to take the time to strengthen your pet's back muscles to accomplish this trick.

Section Two: Hugging You

- Sit in front of your dog and have your dog "sit pretty" and then place his arms on your shoulder saying the verbal command you plan to use for hug. It could be "gimme a hug," or just "hug".
- Give your dog a treat – or use the clicker and treat.
- Say "Okay" to release your dog and help him down.

- Once your pet can hug you from the "sit pretty" position, if he is a larger breed then you can practice with him from a standing position as well.
- The silent signal for Hug is to cross your chest and tap your shoulders with your fingers. You can demonstrate the signal each time you say "Hug." Be patient while teaching this sign language — it may take a while for your dog to make the connection.
- After your pet has learned the signal, then eliminate saying the word "hug" and just give the hand signal for a big hug!

<u>Food for Thought:</u>
Giving a hug is a breed-selective exercise! If you have an injured, dysplastic, or skeletally challenged dog (like a Basset, a Bulldog, or a giant breed) avoid this trick. And don't forget — if your dog refuses, move on to a different trick.

Chapter Thirteen – High Five

Your dog must know how to sit before teaching your pet how to "high five".

Training Tips:

- Have one of your dog's favorite treats held in a closed fist about four or five inches from your pet's nose. Show the hand with the treat to your pet, allowing him to become aware there is a treat in your hand. Wait until your dog begins to paw at your hand.
- Reward your pet once it paws at your hand. This supports the behavior that you are attempting to train. (Don't grab your dogs paw and try to force the high-five.)
- Once your pet begins to paw at your hand, to get the treat, you can begin introducing the high-five command. Instead of presenting a closed fist with the treat held within, offer your hand in the high-five position.
- Wait patiently for your dog to paw your open palm.
- After your pet high-fives your hand, say "high-five" and reward your dog.
- Reduce rewarding with treats. Eventually you will want your dog to high-five on command, without offering a treat first. This can be done over time, by slowly diminishing the amount that you reward your dog with a treat after it high-fives you.

- Diminish the treats slowly until he can high-five without them.
- Over time, replace treats with affection and verbal praise.

<u>Food for Thought:</u>
Make sure you have a quiet place to train your dog. You will want an area that is distraction free. If you keep your pet in a distraction free zone your pet will focus more efficiently and will learn how to high-five quickly. Do not train your dog for more than fifteen minutes at a time. This can cause your dog to become frustrated and hinder training efforts.

Chapter Fourteen- Army Crawl

Your dog will need to know the "down" command prior to doing this trick.
Training Tips:
- Have your dog lie down. Initially when teaching your dog how to craw you will need to have him lie down. This will get him in position and ready to focus on the new trick he is learning
- Have a treat ready to help your dog focus and to reward him with.
- Give the "crawl" command. Once your dog is down, take a few steps in front of him. Squat down and show your dog his treat keeping the treat low to the ground and saying the command "crawl." Your dog should begin to crawl along the ground, trying to get the treat. Reward your dog right away if he crawled correctly.
- If your dog stands up and walks to you, start again from the lying down position, but do not treat him.
- Stay close to you dog at the beginning, if you have too much distance it will be confusing.
- Make sure your dog crawled correctly before rewarding him.
- Now you can increase the distance. Once your dog starts to understand what the "crawl"

command means, you can start to increase the distance your dog crawls. Take your time adding a few steps more each time you train your pet to increase how far your pet can go and reinforce the trick overall.

- Always work slowly to increase the distance your dog is crawling.
- Practice around twice a day.

Food for Thought:
A very important aspect of training your dog is to always reward their good behavior with a treat. This sends a positive message to your dog that a certain behavior was the right thing to do and that he should want to do it again in the future. It is important to keep healthy treats on hand for your training sessions so always make sure you have a healthy treat ready to give to your dog when training. Be careful not to over feed your dog treats. Treats are a great tool to reinforce good behavior. Dogs can eat many healthy treats. Try offering bits of carrot, sweet potato, or a slice of apple.

Chapter Fifteen - Collect garbage

It's a great idea to teach your pet to pick up and put away toys. A variation of this trick is teaching your pet to pick up trash and throw it away.

Training Tips:

- The "drop" command must be learned first.
- Give your pet a piece of trash that they won't be tempted to eat directly over the center of a garbage can and say take it. When he takes it, praise and then give the cue to drop. When she opens her mouth for the treat the trash will fall in the can. Click and treat.
- Once the "drop" is working over the center of the trash can, then move the trash slightly to one side, but still over the can and cue the drop. If it falls into the can click and treat or say good boy (girl). If it doesn't go into the can say "oops" and try again. You will help your dog to understand the trash must go inside the can.
- Once your pet can bring trash you offer her to the can from a distance, start offering it to her closer to the ground, so she must lift it and move to the can.
- Then place the trash on the ground and add a "pick up the trash" cue before you say "Take

it". This will help prompt him to pick up the item and drop in the can.

- Lastly, generalize the cue to a variety of different trash items.

Food for Thought:
Make certain you don't leave valuable objects on the floor when you put in a request for trash pickup! Pets can't make good judgment call about what is trash and what is treasure; your smart phone could end up in the garbage. To add a "wow" to this trick you can get a garbage can with a push-pedal lid. Larger breed dogs can step on the lid to open the can before dropping trash in. If your pet loves garbage this may not be a good idea as more garbage may come out than goes in!

Chapter Sixteen – Skateboard

You will need your dog comfortable on the board. This step must be done slowly and rushing it will hinder your success.

Training Tips:

- Put one paw and then two on the board while it is secured and can't move.
- Get your dog used to being on the board while moving slowly, just a few inches at first and gradually increase. It would be ideal to have all four paws on the skateboard and to also let him move one paw hopping along behind.
- Treat your dog for pushing the board with one or both back paws.
- Gradually work to increase the speed and distance before treating him. Make sure you stay within your dog's comfort zone.
- Loosen the skateboard in stages so that it rocks back and forth, which is needed for steering and go through the entire process with the board at each setting. Spot your dog and make sure he is comfortable while you treat him for rocking back and forth which will help him to ride father.

Food for Thought

Some dogs are athletic, fearless and adventurous enough that skateboarding comes somewhat naturally to them. Other dogs may never reach true proficiency at it, but may enjoy doing it very slowly for brief periods. There are also dogs who are obviously not at all suited to this trick, and if that's the case for your dog, there's no need to even consider attempting to teach him to ride.

Chapter Seventeen – Handstand

Training Tips:
- Put a book on the ground and get your dog to put his back legs on the book. If a book isn't big enough use a larger object. If your dog is having difficulty using the book, use a larger object, that works for your pet. If your dog will not move its feet onto the book, then place your dog's back feet on the book yourself. Treat (or treat and click) when your dog's back feet are on the book.
- Keep doing this step until your dog places its back feet on the book by himself.
- Once your dog is comfortable with placing both its back feet on the book, move the book against the wall. Be reassuring and comforting in your speech.
- Once your pet has not trouble placing his back feet on one book against the wall, slowly begin to increase the height by adding more books. And cue your dog to put his feet on both books. ("up")
- Add a new book every week until the stack is high enough where your dog is using the front part of his body to lift its hind legs to get to the top of the stack of books.

- This step needs to be done very slowly, as your pet is using new muscles and you do not want to risk injury.
- It is not time to remove the books. Once you have added enough books or the object that you have choose, where your dog is nearly vertical when his back feet are placed on the stack of books or object, it is time to remove the books (objece). Have your dog stand in front of the wall, cue the wanted behavior as if the books were still there using your cue word. If you dog makes any effort to get his hind legs onto the wall give him a reward. Keep doing this step until your dog is comfortable placing his hind legs on the wall without any books.
- Finally hold a treat in front of his nose to encourage him to move away from the wall while you support his belly in the "handstand" position.
- Repeat this until your dog can balance on its front legs by itself.

<u>Food for Thought:</u>
This trick takes several weeks to master as it must be done is small increments. Age is a factor. It is best if you wait until your dog is fully grown as an adult before teaching it to do a handstand. Also, if you are trying to teach an older dog, arthritis or other ailments may prevent an older dog from the ability to perform this trick. This trick is best done with a clicker.

Chapter Eighteen - Back Up

Teaching a pet to back up is a handy trick and a lot of fun. It is beneficial if you need your pet to back away from a door, or if he is crowding you. It is also a fun trick to impress your friends!

Training Tips:

- Your dog will need to know the stay command before teaching him to back up.
- Have your dog stay, take a few steps away and then turn to face him.
- Start to move towards your pet, some dogs will step back as soon as you begin walking toward them, if he hasn't yet moved lean your body towards him; if he still hasn't backed up you can push him gently backwards using the command "back up".
- As soon as your dog takes a few steps back, tell him "good" or "yes!" or click your clicker, then give him a treat.
- Keep rewarding your dog each time he backs up on cue.
- Just practice a few minutes each day and before you know it your pet will respond each and every time to the backup command.

Food for Thought:

If your pet gets up and move away instead of going backward when you attempt the steps above, move your dog training sessions to a narrow hallway or other enclosed space. Follow the steps previously given, and make sure that your dog does not have a direction to go except backward. Don't get frustrated if your dog is still not responding as you hoped. Each dog learns differently. Keep training sessions short and positive, usually around ten minutes.

Chapter Nineteen - Open and close doors

Training Tips:
Opening the Door

- Tie a towel or bandana around your door handle. Get your pet to tug on it. (you can get your pet to tug on it by wrapping treats inside, or by playing tug of war with that item prior to tying it on the door handle). When he does, click and treat.
- Keep doing this and begin saying "open" when he pulls the door open (click and treat every time or praise and treat every time.)
- After continual practice, he will be able to open the door.

Close the Door:

- Put a touch stick on the floor or place your hand on the door and get him to come forward.
- When he touches the door moving it slightly click and treat or praise and treat.
- Begin waiting until he has pushed the door all the way closed and use the close cue.
- After repeating the action several times, he should close the door at your command.

Food for Thought:
This command is taught to assistance dogs to help disabled people. This would be very helpful to someone who is wheelchair bound. You must consider the size of your pet before teaching this trick. A door would be too big for a small dog.

Chapter Twenty - Fetch a drink from the Fridge

This is a complicated trick with several steps and will take time and patience to put it all together. Your dog will need to know the fetch and drop command first.

Training Tips:

OPENING THE FRIDGE:

- You will need to tie something (rope, towel, cloth) to your refrigerator door.
- With your pet next to you ask him to "get you a drink" and encourage him to bit on the towel. Praise or click and treat each time the dog bites the towel at your instructions.
- Next say "get me a drink" and encourage your dog to pull on the towel. Praise or click and treat each time he gets the door open.

GRABBING THE BEVERAGE:

- Put the beverage on a shelf that is easiest for your dog to reach it and make sure there is nothing near it.
- To train an empty can would be best. You can play fetch with it earlier, so that your dog is used to grabbing it.
- Prop the refrigerator open for training.
- Point to the can and ask your dog to "fetch" it.
- Then have your dog "drop" it into your hand. Praise or click and treat. Practice this step

until your pet can get you the can using only verbal commands.

- Keep moving further away from the refrigerator and repeat until you are on your couch or where you would normally want him to get you a drink.

CLOSING THE FRIDGE:
- Open the door of the refrigerator just a little.
- Dangle a treat so that your dog leans on his hind legs against the door. Use the "close" command and click and treat or praise and treat when he puts his paws on the door.
- Move a greater distance away, leaving the refrigerator open. Tell your dog to "close". Treat your dog whenever he closes it.

PUTTING IT ALL TOGETHER:
- Stand close to the fridge. Ask your dog to "get me a drink". He should now be comfortable opening the fridge door. While the fridge door is open, tell the dog to "fetch".
- Have him put the drink in your hand and reward him.
- Do the above steps, but this time use the close cue after he grabs the can and treat him and praise him profusely.
- Move further away and say, "get me a drink". You pet should open the fridge door, but if he

forgets any of the steps continue to remind him verbally.

- Always reward him when he brings you the drink. Keep doing this and eventually he will understand that he is to open, fetch, and close the door with the one command "get me a drink".

Food for Thought:
Larger dogs between 12 and 18 months of age are the easiest to teach this cool trick because of their size and willingness to learn, however, it is possible to teach old dogs new tricks, so give it a try! Do not use glass bottles to avoid injury.

Also, keep in mind when teaching this trick that your dog will now know how to open your refrigerator and be able to gain access to the yummy food found in there. Make sure you truly want this ability before teaching this trick

Chapter Twenty-One – Beg

Teaching a pet to beg is a cute trick that is moderately easy to get your dog to do. It just takes a bit of patience on your part. Your pet will need to know the sit command before beginning this trick.

Training Tips:
- While your dog is in the sitting position, hold a treat at his nose and then give the command to "beg".
- As your pet reaches to get the treat, slowly raise the treat over his head so that he must reach up to get to it. Then pull it up until he is sitting on his hind end with his paws up in begging position.
- As soon as your dog has gotten into begging position, praise him and treat, or click and treat.
- Do this routine several times each day for short training intervals. In no time, your dog will be begging on command.

Training in Stages
- Some dogs won't go into begging position in the first training session. You may need to utilize smaller steps. This method is called shaping. The clicker is usually helpful with shaping a behavior.
- Start out with your dog in sitting position.

- Hold the treat in front of his nose and give the cue to "beg".
- Slowly move the treat up so that he is stretching his nose up to reach it.
- Immediately when your dog lifts his nose up, click and tell him "good" and treat him.
- Do this step several times until he is raising his nose in the air each time you give the beg command.
- Next make it just a little tougher. Only click and treat when his nose goes into the air and one of his paws comes off the ground. Repeat until this behavior is consistent when you give the beg command.
- Keep choosing actions that bring your dog closer to getting into the begging position. Practice each behavior until your pet is doing it every time you give the beg command. Eventually your will get to the actual position you are wanting.

<u>Food for Thought:</u>
If you pet makes a mistake more than twice in a row at any stage of the training, don't hesitate to go back to a previous step and train from there. Repetition is the key to learning, make sure your dog is learning the steps correctly.

Chapter Twenty-two – Teaching Your Dog to Find It

The average dog is naturally good at following their nose. They often track things easily and their ability to discover interesting smells can be funneled into a constructive skill with some simple training.

Training Tips:

- Begin by giving the cue word "find" and immediately toss a much-loved treat or favorite toy. Begin easy, by tossing the toy or treat in a flat open area. If your dog doesn't get what you are trying to do, help him by going over to the item, pointing it out etc. When your dog finds the item, then reward him with praise and do the process repeatedly.
- After your dog associates the find cue with retrieving the tossed item, start to make it a little harder for him. Rather than one treat, throw out several treats at the same time. Or hide the toy or hide the treats where your dog cannot see it and have him hunt for it.
- As your dog progresses, you can make the hiding process and more complex. Increase the distance or the difficulty, but don't increase both at the same time. Take it easy and try to make sure your dog is successful and having fun. Always praise your dog enthusiastically every time he brings the toy

back to you and you can reward him with a few rounds of fetch after each successful find.

- Once your dog has a good grasp of the game and is clearly enthusiastic about playing it, you can take the game one step further. Increase the complexity by you or a helper hiding the toy without the dog seeing it done, and then sending the dog in the direction you want him to go. This will mean that he must find the toy on his own. For this to be effective, the dog must understand the command to search and must believe that when you give the command that something is indeed out there for him to find. You must also understand and use the wind. Always send your dog to find the toy from a location downwind of where you have hidden the item.

Food for Thought:
Use meal time to reinforce the "find" command by scattering his kibble on the floor or across an outdoor patio. There is also the option of a food puzzle. These make him work for his food engaging him in both mental and physical exercise.
"Find" can also be a time of playtime or hide-and-seek.

Chapter Twenty-three – Dance

Dancing is a trick that is more easily done by small breed dogs, but the larger breeds can learn to dance with some encouragement and training.

- While your dog is standing hold a beloved treat up over your dog's head. Then give a command such a "up", "dance" or even "spin" until he rises fully on his hind legs. You may need to gently bring both of your arms under his front legs and lift him as you give the cue words so that he understands that you are wanting him up.
- You may need to move the treat just a bit behind your dog's head to get him completely up. Once he is up click and treat, or praise and treat. Continue to do this for several practice sessions until your dog rises on his hind legs easily at the cue word.
- Once your dog has mastered this, then it is a matter of once he is up moving the treat slightly to the left of his head to get him go left and then to the right to get him to go right. Use the cue word, click and praise for any effort in this. As you continue to practice and he easily follows the treat, then begin giving the cue word and giving him the treat after he has accomplished. It is a good idea to have an end cue word such as "release". As

he progresses you can add a spin into the side to side routing.

- If you have a dog that is large and gets excited, be careful when giving him the standup command. Some dogs will use their front paws to push against you for leverage if they get excited and could be problematic if they weight more than you do. Smaller breeds are usually better suited for this trick, but a variety of breed can do this trick with slow methodical training.
- Do training sessions about ten minutes or so, if you or your pet begin to get frustrated, then stop the training session. Go back to a trick that they know well, and make sure you end on a good note. It will take several days to master this trick.

<u>Food for Thought:</u>
This trick is adorable but would not be recommended for dogs that are overweight or for dogs that suffer with hip dysplasia. If you dog has any hip issues or suffers from problems with their hind legs, this trick will put unnecessary strain upon them and should not be taught.

END

Printed in Great Britain
by Amazon